# BOTH FEET IN:

NAVIGATING LIFE IN A FLAMINGO WORLD

PATTI ANN

Illustrated by
TOM JOHNSON

Copyright@2023 Posh Pink Plumes Press
A Direct Subsidiary Imprint of Flying Blue Monkey Press LLC. All rights reserved. No part of this book may be reproduced or used in any manner without the prior written permission of the copyright owner, except for the use of brief quotations in a book review.
For permission, contact the publishing imprint at info@pinkposhplumespress.com

Paperback ISBN: 978-1-7366347-9-0
E-Book ISBN: 978-1-7366347-8-3

First Edition

Edited by Brett Kinsey
Cover Art and Formatting by MJCimageworks
Illustrations and concept ideas by Tom Johnson
Printed in the USA
PoshPinkPlumesPress@
Flying Blue Monkey Press LLC
350 North Leavitt Road, Unit #1271
Amherst, Ohio 44001

www.poshpinkplumespress.com
A subsidiary imprint of
www. flyingbluemonkeypress.com

*This book is dedicated to my grandchildren, who consistently show me that life is full of pink-feather opportunities whenever I choose to walk through it with both feet in.*

*Thank you to Tom Johnson for envisioning the concept of parallel life behaviors between our pink feathered friends and us humans.*

*Thank you to Michael, Brett, Dave, and the Cleveland Writers Group for sharing knowledge, talent, and unwavering support.*

This is a work of fiction. Unless otherwise indicated, all the names, characters, businesses, places, events, and incidents in this book are either the product of the author's imagination or used in a fictitious manner for the story enhancement. Any resemblance to actual persons, living or dead, or actual events is purely incidental.

The flamingo maintains openness for love's choice in partner, regardless of gender, and this book implies the same about relationships and behavioral patterns within the human world. The reader is encouraged to interchange pronouns respectfully depending on preferred character identification. Additionally, the flamingo tends towards a monogamous relationship lifestyle, and although this book takes a humorous look at living life in a flamingo world, it has this goal in mind.

# CONTENTS

*Introduction* — xi

FLAMINGO* — 1
*Flə•mín•gō (noun)*

Welcome — 3
*Flə•mín•gō (noun)*

*Flamingoing — 9
*Flə•mín•gō•iŋ (verb)*

Flamingoing — 13
*The Flamingoing Flaminglet*

*Flamingling — 17
*Flə•mín•gliŋ verb*

Flamingling — 21
*Feather-gathering at its finest.*

*Flamingoed — 29
*Flə•mín•gōd (verb)*

Flamingoed — 31
*Pink Lemonade, Anyone?*

Flamingo Flop — 41
*Flə•mín•gō Fläp (noun)*

Flamingo Flop — 43
*Fearless Flamingo Flopping*

*FLAMINGOER — 51
*Flə•mín•gō•ər (noun)*

The Fearful Flamingoer — 53
*Catalyst for Change*

*Flamazing — 57
*Flə•má•ziŋ (adj)*

Forever Fine-Feathered & FLAMAZING — 61

Both Feet In Glossary — 63
*Life Edition*

Lessons Learned — 67

1. Ten Fun Facts About the Amazing Flamingo — 69

*About the Author* — 71

"One way to get the most out of life is to look upon it as an adventure."

— WILLIAM FEATHER

# INTRODUCTION

There they stood, once again delightfully scattered upon my neighbor's lush, albeit somewhat artificially enhanced, green lawn; the gathering of fabricated, long-legged, brilliantly-pasteled flock members, successfully assisting with the "Newest Addition to the Family" proclamation. Balanced under the summer sun, each fiery flamingo stood sturdy on a single leg, each one a proud pink replication of feathered sun-kissed frolic and fun, poise, and play. In my previous book, *Both Feet In: Navigating Relationships in a Flamingo World,* I spoke of a life-awakening incident involving a similar mob of fake-feathered friends and a sole, pink-feathered dart of awareness making direct contact, resulting in a plumed dose of "AHA."

Staring at those ebony-beaked masters of balance many months ago, I became aware of my propensity to engage in flamingo-style, relationship-seeking behavior as if I were a cardholding, popping-pink member of the web-footed flock. If you recall, a delightful, flamingo-led exploration of some correlating flamingo and human behavioral patterns ensued. Undoubtedly, each of us rightfully earned an honorary, pink-feathered flock member badge for completing that fun yet eye-opening literary adventure, and we made a new pastel-popping fine-feathered friend along the way.

Anyway, I digress. It's just that the pink, plastic, one-legged, perfectly-stoic, stationary flock-gathering, suddenly triggered the delightful memory. I refocused on the road ahead and gently released my foot off the brake pedal. I was eager to arrive home, change from work attire into comfy pink flamingo-dotted sweats, and relax with an umbrella-topped, refreshing, sugary, foo-foo beverage in hand. That *was* the plan until a flash of pink movement captured my side-eye attention. Okay, yes, it had been a long day at work. More precisely, it had been a tedious week of stressful days, and I was tired; however, there was no mistaking it. A pink imposter was precariously posing among this flock. Either *that* or I was in dire need of an updated eye exam.

The noise from the sudden, not-so-gentle press on the brake pedal - okay, I may have loudly slammed that black rectangular pad of stoppage - resulted in a single, pink neck slowly lifting. Direct eye-to-side-eye-connection occurred, familiar recognition occurred, and pink flamingo panic set in. The excited feather ruffling sent wisps of pink flying plumes into the air.

I was right!

I could amuse you with details of the following fifteen minutes - the car door opening then slamming shut, the ensuing chase among fabricated pink birds with human footfalls closing in on webbed steps, the backward neck-craning glances, and just as I felt the plumed pink sleek softness beneath my fingers, the successful lift-off, wings spread wide, spindly legs tucked in tightly, webbed feet dangling and beak pointing south - but I won't.

I stood, greatly perplexed, surrounded by the mass of stoic, pink plastic replicas, and watched the pink blob disappear southward before thinking about scanning for any other lurkers among the now-suspicious flock. I do admit to wading through the fake flamboyance, gently touching each shiny head to ensure no other imposters remained, for I needed no additional surprises. My human blood-pumper could handle only so much.

I want to think that I'm an intelligent member of the human species, so I knew better than to venture a guess as to the purpose of the pink-feathered flamingo's undercover incognito mission, *and* I knew better than to assume that the behavior of humans was once again under examination. I knew better than to "assume" initially, but humans tend to do that anyway...and I'm human. Besides, it would be ridiculous to think that there could be any additional correlation between human behavior and that of a flamingo!

Completely ridiculous.

Right?

Hmm, or is it?

I ducked just in time for the pink-plumed-top dart of awareness to skim by instead of making direct contact. I had learned the fine art of neck-maneuvering during the last visit to the world of flamingos, and I was well aware that those darts may be fancy and pretty, but they're also painful. Missed contact or not, once again, the delivery of stunning, eye-opening realization landed squarely on the intended target, resulting in a direct bullseye on my human brain. What had I been thinking? Could it be that I had engaged in one-legged balancing, energy-conserving, comfort-causing, change-resistant flamingoing behaviors, not only for relationship-seeking but possibly in other ways?

Have I been doing this my entire life? Could it be that YOU have as well?

Now, now. Don't get your human feathers all ruffled again. Breathe deep, and allow me to explain.

Better yet, let's ask a flamingo...again.

# FLAMINGO*
## FLƏ•MÍŊ•GŌ (NOUN)

A bird extraordinaire. Avian specimen of pink perfection. Exemplification of balance and poise. Portrayer of glitz and fun. "Spokesbird" for all things tropical, sunny, and warm. Utilized as an adornment for celebratory occasions and just about anything else the human species can conceive. In other words, the envy of the avian world, and rightfully so.

*Webb-sters Life Edition Dictionary

# WELCOME
## FLƏ•MÍŊ•GŌ (NOUN)

Hello there! It's lovely to see you again, although the unfortunate catalyst for this meeting was highly unexpected. No worries; all is not lost. Here in the world of feathered fuzziness, there is always a pink lining to silver clouds. This unanticipated interaction resulted in a much-needed revamping of the Flamingo Handbook of Undercover Operations. More precisely, page thirty-two, paragraph three, line five - a line needing clarification regarding all undercover flamingo missions and the one-legged-standing mandate always to remain still, REGARDLESS HOW TASTY THAT LAWN INSECT APPEARS TO BE!!!

But then again, we are only flamingos, and like members of the human species, we also make mistakes here in pink-feathered paradise. Yes, I know it's hard to believe, given our incomparable awesomeness. And, yes, our mistakes are a little more fun as they occur in a warm climate (you humans can keep your feather-freezing temperatures), involve lots of water and splashing, and often result in fluttering pink feathers in flight. And who can help but smile when popping pink feathers start floating in the air?

What's that?

Ah, yes.

Sorry for the lengthy explanation. You're curious why this good-looking, pink, fine-feathered, black-beaked, one-legged balancing flamingo was hanging out in a human yard among a fabricated pastel life-like avian flock? You do know what they say about curiosity, don't you?

Psst, come closer.

Please realize that if the first book didn't enlighten you, this curiosity might lead to something you aren't ready to hear. If you've forgotten, some of you aren't exactly fond of this thing called change. See, the rest of my pink-plumed posse and I have been watching you and the rest of your two-legged friends. Yes, I know you thought *you* were the spectators all this time. Not so, "humanhopper." It's the other way around. The entire flamingo population is keenly aware and greatly intrigued by the ongoing love affair you humans have with our pink-feathered society - hence the undercover flamingo mission.

That said, I fully understand this adoration of all things flamingo. And who can blame you? I highly doubt smiling crowds would gather to watch *you* balancing on one leg. Well, perhaps there is a slim chance it could happen if you did it wearing a costume of pink feathered fluffiness; not quite the same effect, but undoubtedly, a sight to see! I'm just saying there's a reason we draw the crowds. We represent sunshine, tropical lands, silliness and serenity, giddiness, and grace. It's why you hire our clones to stand on your lawns, broadcasting the latest human accomplishment. It's why some of you decorate your homes in pink, spindly-legged, feathered décor and wear flamingo-dotted matching shorts and shirts. As an aside, the boxer briefs are taking it a bit too far, guys, although I give you a feathered high-five wing slap for the great taste in strategic patterning.

Human, please understand.

There's more to this unrelenting attraction that you have with us. While you may now understand the human/flamingo behavioral connection regarding relationship-seeking – *if* you read the previous book – you may still be overlooking the possibility that the correlation of behaviors runs deeper.

It's okay. I didn't recognize it at first, either. It was only after many hours of intense people-watching that I became awakened. Okay, are you ready for this? The connection between human and flamingo is more encompassing than the muck currently surrounding my single, sunken, webbed foot, and since we are on the subject of feet, I have a question for you. Have you ever wondered why we stand on one foot?

I know you have.

It's a well-known human belief that "curious minds want to know," so please allow me to share some flamingo facts with you. We don't engage in one-legged standing just because it looks cool, which it does. Instead, this posturing is a vital component of our societal behavior. We stand on one foot because it's more comfortable while also allowing the conservation of heat and energy. Of course, those aren't the only two reasons, but they are crucial in this human-flamingo connection I speak of.

Hmm, not putting both feet down - or in - because sometimes that balancing act is just more accepted, familiar, safe, and cozy.

Sound familiar?

The good part for us is that nobody questions why flamingos do it.

The real question is, why are YOU doing it?

How often have you found yourself hesitant to try something new? Are you generating questionable reasons for not following your passion or making a change? Have you become so mired in the pond of uncertainty, precariously balancing on one foot because you're concerned with what others may say or think? Are you finding it increasingly comfortable to remain standing with one foot deep and grounded while keeping the other foot tucked up snugly in the comfortable inertia of indecision? Hesitant to risk your balance?

Now, before you arrive, indignantly splashing in this pond of reflected recognition, let me remind you that I've heard some excuses justifying this behavior. "What if nobody accepts me?" "I'm too old to start over." "I'm too young to be taken seriously." "Everyone will think I'm crazy." "Only twenty more years until retirement." "I don't want to fail." "It always ends the same way, so why bother trying?" "But, but, but ... I don't like change."

Now, we're getting down to the nitty-gritty of the matter once again.

I reiterate: Humans aren't always overly fond of this process called change or of decision-making. Full disclosure: Neither are we flamingos, and it's why I state we have more in common than you think. For your information, "life" also happens here in the world of flamingos.

Please allow me to reiterate the potential problem with this resistance to change; continually maintaining the one foot in - one foot out - behavior may halt forward movement and stop you from living your best passion-led life. The result is permanent, stuck-in-the-mud residence among the human equivalent of a pink one-legged tribe of "anything but free" yet remarkably looking fanciful flamingos. Eventually, that may become slightly tedious - or not - as I have previously stated. It depends on how well you wear brilliant pink feathers and remain balanced on one foot.

Beautiful human, I'm here to help you figure it all out. We got this.

Welcome to my world once again.

No need to worry. I'll remain by your side.

We can't have you wandering around this watery oasis alone, right?

Just watch the feathers. Must I remind you how long it takes to get an appointment with Fabio at Fanciful and Fine Feathers Salon and Spa in Fernandina? I thought the wait was long before; however, he has gained some notoriety. I'm just saying.

# *FLAMINGOING
FLƏ•MÍŊ•GŌ•IŊG (VERB)

The expected avian behavior for all flamingo flock members. An innate propensity to remain in the one-legged stance of comfortable familiarity for long periods. Collective and societal patterning of unnecessary movement resistance once a graceful one-legged balance occurs unless necessary for fundamental provisions and daily flamingo interaction. This behavior ensures warmth retention, a sense of familiar comfort, and conservation of energy spent on unnecessary movement. As with all behavioral patterns, flamingoing may become problematic if resistance to forward movement occurs due to fear of failure, past negative experiences, and reluctance to take chances, resulting in missing out on full-spectrum living, an event undesirable for all species, feathered or not.

**Lesson #1:** Remaining in stagnant waters affects emotional and physical health. Besides, it may entirely dim one's brilliant plumage!

"Waters get choppy sometimes. It's just part of life in a flamingo world. You best learn to handle both the gentle ripples and the stronger waves."

— EIDER ELDER

# FLAMINGOING
## THE FLAMINGOING FLAMINGLET

Growing up as a flamingo, I knew no other way of life. From my first shrieking honk, the pink feathered flock membership arrived with specific innate flamingoing characteristics and behaviors. I am reasonably sure that natural behaviors accompanied the first human infant wail as well. As a young chick, surrounded daily by the brilliant pink plumage of my parents and siblings, my early years were everything a baby flamingo could ever need: nest snuggling with mom as she honked tales from another infamous parental avian figure, pond splashing in the mangrove's wading section with my friends, testing my father's patience while perfecting a wide range of honks and grunts, teetering web-footed waddling, feather counting, and the fine art of beak polishing. Life was better than an algae-laden pond of fresh shrimp, and that's saying a lot!

I believed my color-filled life would continue ripple-free and absent of upsetting waves at that young age. But then again, I was young and didn't know better. I still had many lessons to learn. I hadn't even mastered the fine art of balance yet; however, that second year of life was about to arrive in feathered-belly-flopping style.

I was an early bird. Long before my feathered toddler-sized friends, I had accomplished the tail shake, the web-footed run, the preening process involved in feather maintenance, and even the M.J. strut (reverse web-footed walking, if you didn't know). I was proud, and many a-wing pointed in my direction with admiration, which was great. But, I had yet to accomplish the most crucial flamingo rite of passage, which drove me loon-y. The envy-triggering, awe-inspiring, perfectly balanced, knee-locked, one-legged stance continued to elude me!

Now, I never questioned the purpose of this flamingo milestone. I just wanted to do it because every other flamingo in my flamboyance was doing it, and well, of course, I wanted to be just like "them."

You wouldn't know anything about that line of thinking, would you?

Hmm.

Anyway, I remember the day it happened. I made my way to the pond just like every other day, walked a few feet into the water, and lifted one skinny leg, tucking one tiny, webbed foot up under my feathers, my other leg shaking slightly in an attempt to maintain some semblance of balance. This wasn't the first time I attempted this feat of feet magic; it was more like the seventy-ninth. Each time previously, my tiny, pink-plumed body would teeter, totter, and then topple into the reflective water of coolness, sending up droplets of self-perceived failure. And it never failed that a few of my "so-called" fellow flaminglet flock members would honk slightly in amusement behind their closed beaks each time this occurred.

I believe the true lesson began then. However, I didn't understand or care at that time. I just wanted to stand one-legged like all the other flamingos. And I was determined! I recall every moment of that notorious day as if in a motion picture playing at slow speed. I was standing in water that barely reached my bottom tail feather, slightly adjusting my body to the left and a little to the right. I remember the feeling of serendipitous balance, the moment when everything felt perfectly aligned in my watery world. I remember looking down at my reflected self, perfectly balanced, wings spread wide, feathers slightly shifting in the warm tropical breeze. I can recall the sounds of my parents' honks, white plumes lifting in the air, and their necks craning in ways I didn't know possible. It was a fantastic feeling.

Until Freddy, the local flamboyance bully, shuffled over and side-swiped my perfectly balanced leg, karate-flaminglet style, sending me splashing into the cool water, resulting in a bevy of chuckling grunts and honks from some of the fine feathered flock. So much for the adage about birds of a feather sticking together.

It was okay, though. I was young, and life in the tropics went on. I eventually became quite the balancer (constantly glancing around for Freddy first, of course.) If being accepted as a flamingo meant balancing, I would be the best balancer I could be. There was no way I ever wanted to hear those teasing honks of self-perceived failure again.

Ahh, the lessons we learn before understanding the importance and impact of each feathery plume of life experience. The balance. The rise and the fall. The soar and the splash.

Here, have a feather, as I have plenty. I'm sure you have your fair share of earned plumes of wisdom yourself. Let's continue, shall we? I've some tales to tell.

. . .

**Lesson #2:** The most priceless flamingo feathers are those obtained through consistent resurfacing after life's unexpected splashes.

# *FLAMINGLING
## FLƏ•MÍŊ•GLIŊ VERB

Every connection with other webbed puffs of pink throughout all life stages. Interflamingling and intraflamingling exchanges encompass all modes of communicating with similar species and involve flamingo-alized nasal honks, variations of pastel wing flapping, and slight nuances in neck-craning.

One's flamingling behavior is entirely dependent, influenced, and affected by the many dives and dips taken in the ever-changing waters found in Life's Lagoon.

"You are not a drop in the ocean...
   You are the entire ocean in a drop."

— RUMI

# FLAMINGLING
## FEATHER-GATHERING AT ITS FINEST.

As I recall, it was one of my earliest flaminglet flamingling experiences of social interaction, and it occurred at Miss Ada's Avian School on the first day of preschool. Having spent the previous four years fine-feather-tuning my vast flamingo skill set, I was excited and over-eager to attend the school like all the other chick members of the pink-feathered flamboyance. The goal? I wanted endless fun with the pastel-plumed friends I splashed with throughout the recent summer months.

I strutted through the reedy marsh over to the neighboring pond on that first day of lagooned learning, clutching the newly purchased (five clams worth!) shrimp and algae-logoed lunch bucket in one wing and holding on to my mother's outstretched span of feathers with my other wingtip. Refreshed and confident, beak polished with a dab of ebony-enhancing wax, my top feathers strategically positioned and held securely with popping pink pomade promising long-lasting hold, I kept my bevy of full plumes held high as we set off to the preschool.

What could go wrong? My mother had even allowed a

quick spray of my father's Agua di Avi cologne. I was styling! However, what I *wasn't* doing was paying attention to my mother's grunts and lowered honks until the view of the school nest came into view.

"Remember, there will be many new flaminglets to have fun with."

My side eyes looked at her, my neck craned in confusion, and my feathers popped free from underneath the pink pomade (so much for secure hold!). I honked in confusion.

What did she mean?

Wait. What?

She continued honking and grunting, but my bird brain didn't want to acknowledge what I heard! There would be newly feathered flamingo flaminglets at preschool? Wasn't it going to be just my best friends and me?

Nearing the water-logged school of learning, I saw some familiar friends, and my avian heart leaped. I also saw Freddie, the bully from my earlier pond years, and my avian heart belly splashed beneath my body of feathers. I tightened the grip on my mother's wing so firmly that feathers became entangled, and my mother had to pat down the loose ones. This feeling felt foreign; I had no idea why my little pastel heart was pounding so hard. And then I remembered. I remembered the forgotten incident in the pond a year ago, the group laughter, the momentary feeling of not belonging, and my concern that I wouldn't fit in.

Standing at the preschool nest entrance, I withdrew one webbed foot up under my fluff of comfort and refused to move while simultaneously honking and grunting pleas for an immediate retreat. Side-eyes turned, and although several other pink feathered bodies honked similar appeals (including some from Freddy, my pink-plumed nemesis), I knew that all those eyes focused on me.

My mother, pink-pearled necklace dangling from her sinewy neck, bent down and looked at me, side-eye to side-eye. "You are flamazing, and I pink wingtip promise you will be fine." I didn't listen, and my honks intensified in urgency while, at the same time, my neck threatened to knot itself into a perfect pastel algae-tasting pretzel.

It didn't appear to matter to my mother. She straightened up, and as difficult as I'm sure it was, she disconnected our entangled feathers, shook out her plumed fluff, and webfoot padded away. Ms. Ava, fully aware of the situation, waddled over, reached down for a wing, and led me into the school while drops of liquid salt rolled down my feathers to the soft ground below.

I made four new friends that day.

It was a pattern that often repeated during my childhood and early adolescence. That same initial hesitancy occurred at each academic pond level upgrade and every time I entered a new classroom for the first time. The insecurity resurfaced when I joined the first-year fledgling football team, at my first coed Flamenco Fiesta, on my first date, and on many more occasions.

And I made many new friends while learning the essential skills of interflamingling and intraflamingling along the way. I learned how to resurface after flamingo flops and how to float when tired of battling unexpected waves. I learned the flamingo flirt and how to flamingo flamenco with the best of them!

Unfortunately, I also learned the fine art of pretending along the way. Whenever the insecurity, hesitancy, or fear would surface, I'd recall the comfort of warm, familiar, safe, feathered fluff, and deep below the reflective watery surface, I allowed my webbed foot to climb to familiar territory with nary another flamingo being aware. That innate skill of secret one-legged balancing became an easy excuse for dealing with the life changes I found uncomfortable. But it was unacceptable, for that's not how life is lived in a flamingo world, remember? We live both feet in. So, what was an insecure fluff of pink feathers supposed to do?

The answer arrived during a solo briny shrimp expedition taken to clear my pink feathered head and provide reflection upon the meaning of my avian life. I was practicing for my first job as a pond guard in a neighboring flamboyance, and I felt some insecurity seeping in. Standing in the refreshing wetness, balancing like a pro on one sturdy leg, the other leg strategically folded for comfort, I looked down towards the liquid surface. There, moving at anything *but* a snail's pace, was the largest, tasty-looking, multiple-legged crustacean I had ever seen on the pond floor.

That's not all I saw, however, and as the tasty creature scuttled away, my mother's image briefly appeared on the reflective surface of liquid wisdom. The imagined vision remained only briefly but long enough for me to remember the three words she whispered in my ear so many years ago while standing at the preschool door, my wingtip desperately holding onto her feathered span. The recalled honks now invisibly floated past my wispy auriculas (ears for you, human folk) and made their way into my pink, bird-brain memory banks.

I remembered, and at once, those grunts made sense and found their home within my pastel heart, unlocking that innate "knowing," arriving at the perfect time.

My mom was right!

I was flamazing!

Why was I thinking any different?

For the next several minutes, time stood still as the tropical sun shone down on the blue water's surface, my pastel image shattering into a mesmerizing sea of reflective truth shards. And then, without realizing it was happening, my safe and securely tucked webbed foot slowly slid down, not stopping until next to its sunken orange twin.

At that moment, life made sparkling sense. I felt unstoppable and powerful enough to rule all ponds, lagoons, lakes, and oceans that I wade in, waves and all. My confidence returned. I had a whisk to my waddle and an oomph to my tail-feathered walk. From that moment on, I strutted with both feet into the unfamiliar, the new experience, the exciting activity I was curious about, the weekly social event.

In that instant, I understood that although it may be easier to balance in one-legged comfort, I couldn't allow that single webbed foot to remain in the mire of fear and insecurity for one more minute. I needed to put both feet in.

And it worked. Not only was I hired as a lifeguard, but I earned the top perch of protection. Life was pink and rosy, comfy and cozy.

At least for a year or so.

And then adulthood came splashing into my pond of serenity, testing my ability to ride out the waves. That's just how life flows, whether you're a flamingo or a human. It's a good thing we flamingoes have water-repellent feathers!

"But where, after all, would be the poetry of the sea were there no wild waves?"

— JOSHUA SLOCUM

## *FLAMINGOED
FLƏ•MÍŊ•GŌD (VERB)

This "unpleasant" event occurs when the churning waters relentlessly refuse to provide a calm and ripple-free haven for maintaining a secure flamingo balance despite putting your best foot forward. These unfortunate yet unavoidable occurrences will repeatedly happen during a flamingo's lifespan and occur in the work pond, during goal-seeking, within pink puff flamingo relationships, and when the tropical skies turn stormy for no apparent reason. Sometimes, it triggers a desire to throw pink wings up and shuffle swiftly into the Pond of Pity. Sometimes, it leads to an unexpected Flamingo Flop. Although many pink flamingos view being flamingoed as a negative and unwanted cloud of frustration, these same two-legged balancers are often surprised by the hidden pastel lining.

**Lesson # 3** When life tosses you a lemon, remember, nothing tastes sweeter than a coconut shell full of pink lemonade ... oh, and top it off with a tropical-looking drink umbrella!

# FLAMINGOED
## PINK LEMONADE, ANYONE?

While it's usually not a pleasant experience here in the pink world, being "flamingoed" in the human world can be an experience of great joy. I can't blame you, either. Who wouldn't feel a quickening of the heart and unspeakable joy at the sight of a popping, pink flamingo flock adorning their yard, proclaiming another human year has passed, or announcing to the world that another human child has joined the family? And if you "beings of walking flesh" would liven up a bit, we may consider throwing a plastic human replica or two up in the mangrove to celebrate a feathery hatch or a hitch ... just something for you to consider.

That's not the "flamingoed" I'm referring to here. I'm talking about those times in life when you think you're heading for a smooth landing on a liquid runway of "smooth as glass" water, and you end up crashing in a flamingo flop of the worst magnitude, sending up waves of salty water in the aftermath. It's not a pretty sight; speaking from experience, it impacts something much more precious than a feathered body. It affects the ego. Yes, even we flamingos can suffer from bruised pride, although ours do turn a much more attractive shade of purple, almost magenta.

From what I've gathered during my secret undercover missions in the human world, I'm sure you can relate to the ebb and flow, the rise and fall, the swan dive and the feathered-covered belly flop. How one handles it, though, depends entirely on the feathers of wisdom you gather while immersed in Life Lagoon.

Ready for a deeper dive into the murky waters of life lessons?

Do you need anything before we begin?

A fluffing of the nest?

Perhaps some freshly squeezed pink lemonade served in a coconut shell?

No? You good?

Okay. Here we go. Remember the day I perfected my one-legged balance in the neighborhood pond? Do you remember Freddy, the flaminglet bully who sneakily sideswiped my precariously balanced leg? Flamingoed! It was my first-ever experience of feeling on top of the highest sand bar and then experiencing the immediate aftermath of questioning my sense of worth. I compared myself to all the other flock members who had witnessed the act of Karate Flaminglet destruction. It happened fast, and I had no idea those feelings existed.

That was just the beginning. It would happen many more times. I remember trying out for the lead actor in the drama club production of *One Soared Over the Flamingo's Nest*. If you recall, I regained my self-esteem that last year of high school after integrating my mother's wise honks of wisdom into everyday feathered life. So, it was no surprise to all my pink-plumed nestmates when I strutted into that audition without a doubt that the lead role was already mine. I had rehearsed my lines, perfected the crazy side-eye glare, and tousled my top feathers with enough pink pomade to keep those loose feathers in position. I could already envision the wave of pink wings flapping in awe of the performance just witnessed, the honks and grunts echoing against the amphi-nest walls, the unison stomping of webbed feet in a quest for an encore.

Uh, yeah. I didn't get the lead role.

Guess who did?

Yep, Freddie.

So began a slow and steady accumulation of imagined pink slips of flamingo-al rejection, ones I pretended to fluff off. Now, don't get me wrong. Remember, I had attended acting class, and as quickly as those inner honks of doubt began to creep back into my avian brain, I just as promptly acted as if everything was okay. Besides, the Pond of Pity was always there, offering needed reflection a mere waddle away, and I did my fair share of waddling and Pond of Pity pondering.

Perhaps the most remarkable example of being flamingoed I can offer is the time, early into my adulthood, when I had orange-webbed-foot padded into the much-anticipated yearly Mangrove Mixer with my side-eyes-sight set on seeking something new and exciting. Please bear with me as I reiterate this brief tale of love and loss for those readers unfamiliar with this tragic tale.

I had grown weary of sameness, felt I was treading water, and desired to dip my webbed foot into the dating pond of pink-feathered potential once again. Nothing seemed to be changing, and although we flamingoes don't have much to complain about living in a pink tropical paradise, something just seemed missing, yet I couldn't place my wingtip on what that was. Besides, D.J. Flame was spinning the tracks that evening at the long-awaited event, and my "wingmen" were as eager as I to engage in some tailfeather-shaking flamencoing.

I made my way to the water's edge that evening, an aura of confidence trailing in the warm summer breeze. My confidence was high. My ebony bill shone in sleek glossiness, and the expensive pink Avi Di Agua pomade kept my feathers perfectly positioned. I was so color-coordinated even my pastel reflection glasses matched my popping pink body of fluff to perfection.

It was going to be an evening to remember! I imagined all necks craning and turning in my direction as I located the perfect viewing spot and waded into the watery swamp of potential pink partnership that warm summer evening. I positioned myself into the standard flamingo stance with one foot sunken deep in the warm muck below and tucked my other foot into my warm, feathered body. Looking around the watery scene, I nudged up the pastel surveyors of potential plumed puffs of perfection and glanced at what I imagined would be diverse possibilities.

It was at that moment I earned another feather of wisdom. One can't always trust the view from behind rose-colored glasses.

In the following few minutes, awareness seeped into my brain. Surrounding me was just one more flamboyance, similar to all the rest, of one-legged balancers who were hesitant to take chances, reluctant to test new waters, and suspicious of making an unfamiliar and potentially uncomfortable splash. It felt hopeless! I would never find the unique pink soulmate destined for future partnered nest-building. They were all the same! What was wrong with these fellow flamingos!?

Self-awareness doesn't always come quickly.

Figuring I could perhaps ease my dismay with a scuttling briny shrimp, I looked down at the water's reflective surface and caught sight of the wavering image of my single sunken webb.

Hmm, wait a minute.

Could it possibly be?

Had I become the next generation of unquestioning societal flamingo behavior? I'm afraid so. As reluctant as I was to admit it, I grew increasingly comfortable with familiarity. I was in a rut, a squishy one, but a rut, nonetheless. No wonder I felt something was missing. I was turning into my parents, Great Being of all Things Pink forbid!

I experienced a refreshed determination to break free from the flock at that moment. Nothing changes if nothing changes, right? I shook out my feathers, slowly slid my foot from where it nestled, placed it deep into the murk below, and readjusted my newfound two-legged balance. Flamingos generally go with the flock flow; any behavior deviance is sometimes enough to create a literal splash. I didn't know what to expect, but I knew what had to happen.

I had been so concerned about causing disruption, swimming upstream when all the others floated downstream, and sending masses of errant feathers flying into the air that I forgot just to be me. I had once again forgotten that I was uniquely flamazing. And that's what matters. Regardless of the outcome, whether a perfect-ten high dive or a messy flamingo flop, I was going for it!

Talk about imagined immediate manifestation! The entire pink paradise aligned itself at that moment. I pivoted in my watery surroundings, and against the moonlit night, I espied an aura of hazy pink from across the mangrove. Something was happening! Could it be that easy? Would instant rewards appear that quickly if I moved in a new direction?

I saw my destiny across the wet surface, and the hushed (I had rendered them honkless by my little act of rebellion) flock parted. There stood a puff of perfection, long eyelashes topping dark side-eyes, precisely positioned pink feathers, a beak that reflected the moonlight, and tail feathers tastefully blinged; all that was honk-stopping in itself! Even more impressive was that this pink plumed ava stood on *both* legs, not balancing on one leg like the others!!

It was destiny!

It had to be!!

Wading two-footed through the dark waters, tiny pink-winged Cupid flamingos fluttering above my head with their passion-filled pink arrows ready to release, thoughts of potential long-term nesting, nights of neck-craning and feather snuggling, and even the possibility of tiny mini-me's running around the nest, filled my feathered-encased brain. I'll spare you all the mushy details of the next two hours. However, there was plenty of mutual neck-craning, tail feather bopping, and wingtip holding as we shook pastel plumes to D.J. Flame and tiny pink arrows dotting the darkened moonlit sky above us.

Ah, sweet little story, isn't it?

Until the fifth date, when I arrived at the nest of my pink-plumed, fluffy-feathered, future nest-builder. The nest door opened to the sight of a single webbed foot tucked halfway up against a balanced leg beneath the feathered pink plumes. Sure, the ensuing excuses seemed plausible as she honked them out; not enough time, overstressed, "It's not you, it's me." However, it didn't ease the heartbreak to come.

Yes, it was true.

*BOTH FEET IN:*

I had been flamingoed again.

I handled the rejection reasonably well, having made several previous trips to the Pond of Pity and earning more than a few feathers from surfing the waves in Life Lagoon. I flew away with beak pointed north, and feathered head held high. It wasn't easy, though, and it's enough to ruffle anyone's feathers, flamingo or not!

Navigating this journey called life is tricky, and it will nose-dive you from every direction regardless of whether your feet are sunken below a liquid surface or placed firmly on solid ground. You just need to become better at ducking the dives and riding the waves. It's all about the balance, "humanhopper" friend of mine. Balance. Ebb and Flow.

Oh, what's that? You want to know what a flamingo flop is? You got it!

In the meantime, remember, balance! You'll need it for this one.

Lesson #4: Sometimes it's just a matter of adjusting your wings ... oops ... sails.

"You must live in the present, launch yourself on every wave, find your eternity in each moment. Fools stand on their island of opportunities and look toward another land. There is no other land; there is no other life but this."

— HENRY DAVID THOREAU

# FLAMINGO FLOP
FLə•MÍŋ•GŌ FLÄP (NOUN)

An unavoidable life event that happens to all species members at some point if living life in forwarding motion. A natural result of taking chances. This can occur at any time and may occur within many life dynamics, including relationship-seeking, skill-building, business ventures, or when one is willing and daring enough to seek new adventures. Happens when the imagined smooth "*that* deserves a 10" ripple-free swan dive into clear waters becomes an unexpected belly flop into unfamiliar waters, most often resulting in an unanticipated watery mess. Sometimes used as an excuse for sedentary flamingoing or flamingoer behavior. Masquerades as some of the most valuable feather-earning life lessons a flamingo can experience, such that recognition of the downside risk(s) may deliver full flamingo maturity status.

**Lesson** #5: Sometimes, the most valuable pearls hide inside the roughest clams.

# FLAMINGO FLOP
## FEARLESS FLAMINGO FLOPPING

I know it sounds a bit intimidating. Smooth dives are one matter, but a watery flop from any height may seem unwelcoming and result in a painful soaking! In the author's first book, which focused on relationship-seeking in a Flamingo World, the flamingo flop involved the churning waters of potential relationship partnering. The Webb-sters "Life" Version Dictionary covers more ground when defining the parameters of a more generalized *life* feathered belly, water splashing, flop.

Regardless of the differences, one point remains consistent when taking any chance that may result in the dreaded flamingo flop. It occurs because there is an unrelenting need to answer the heart's call, an inner pull, a passion that won't relent, an inner itch that surpasses all logic or previous outcome memory.

A flamingo flop is always a possibility when living "both feet in" and taking a chance at experiencing a potential life-changing downpour. Can you possibly imagine how dull and ripple-free the lake of life would be if one never risked – *come a little closer* – failure?

Pretty nice, huh?

There would be no worries about an undertow, no concerns about water-drenched feathers, no potential for bruised egos or shattered pink pumpers. It would feel like floating on "inertia-d" liquid. No lulling bumps of waves to fill you with expectation, no exhilarating, unexpected "life is fantastic" crash of waves, no skill-building surfing, no laughter-triggering splashing ... ever.

Umm ... NO thank you very much!!

Yes, I've had my share of feather-drenching flops. You've probably had your fair share of them, too. Okay, maybe not ones that have left your feathers drenched because you have none, but you know what I mean.

May I share a secret?

I wasn't always the wise feathered balancer you see before you.

I know, I know. It's hard to believe.

As an adult, I still find myself teetering, tottering, toppling, and flopping along the fluid channel of this voyage called life, just like that little flaminglet learning the skill of one-legged balance. The splash is just louder. I don't know about you humans, but we flamingos aren't gifted some magical, pretty pink manual for living life at birth. It would make matters easier, perhaps, but I'm not sure that knowing every outcome and destiny would make life the exciting adventure it should be.

Allow me to share some of my most memorable flops.

Remember Freddy, the local flamboyant bully? The solitary memory of that Karate Flaminglet leg swipe provided the catalyst to send me web-footed wading into the Academy of Ava Achievement and Feather Attainment early in my teenage years. And that happened only because my fine-feathered parents finally lifted their wings in exasperated surrender after days of exchanged honking and guttural grunting. I also had to promise my parents I would nest sit with my younger sister when needed, but it was worth it. I was more than excited to receive my membership badge for the Pink Plume Power-Up Program, which touted the delivery of a skill that would build triple-strength leg muscle in ten days. TEN DAYS!!

My long spindly legs — soon to be the envy of all other flamingos — hit the straw floor as soon as the yellow globe of tropical warmth rose just above the "Welcome to Pink Paradise" billboard sign. Every morning, I grabbed a cup of pink plankton Chowderade and headed out the nest door with determination and motivation filling my pink, plumed puff of a body. With each webbed foot flop, I envisioned the ebony bills of my peers dropping agape in awe. I imagined their feathers ruffling in adoration and honks filling the air with admiration instead of the behind-the-tailfeather snickers that continued to resound inside my pink feathered head.

And every day on the mirrored surface of the Academy's liquid surroundings, I willed my reflection to sprout massive muscles quickly and magically. I squatted, planked, and lunged. I dipped, dove, and sprinted. Sweat rolled off my feathers like oil on water. I practically saw those sinewy leg muscles expanding. And they did, by one-eighth of an inch on each leg. Nobody was to blame except me because I should have read the fine print. I skimmed over the minuscule words stating "results may vary" based on individual body structure, diet, and continued exercise outside the Academy. I tried to make sense of the lack of expected results. I reasoned that I *was* still in the peak teenage growing phase, that algae and shrimp *were* at my wingtips every day, and besides, how was I supposed to know that video games didn't count as "exercise?"

But I had tried so hard. I had given it my all while I was there.

Nevertheless, I flamingo-flopped.

Well, that's how it felt. I didn't even get a refund. However, I did receive a professional-looking popping pink certificate proclaiming completion of the Pink Plume Power-Up Program *and* a merit feather for another life lesson learned. The important point was that I had tried. I had put my best foot — well, feet — forward and risked failure. And you should see the muscles on these legs now. I'm not boasting but look at these thigh muscles!

I just needed to learn about patience.

Anyway, my human friend, I know you've had your share of similar lessons. I've witnessed times when you put all effort in and performed at your peak level, which still ended in a messy splash. If I were to count the number of times I endured a flamingo flop, I would run out of feathers. The earlier Mangrove Mixer story wasn't the last time I experienced a pink shattered avian heart. I flamingo-flopped my way several more times in pursuit of a potential pink partnership that didn't take flight.

But I continued to risk it.

There was a time when I wanted to be the next Pink Picasso and signed up for the Paint Like Picasso art class. According to the teacher, the blobs of spattered pastel looked more like squashed pink plankton than the attempted self-portrait and didn't merit a passing grade. It's okay. It just wasn't meant to be, besides, it's not my best talent.

But I took the chance.

And how about the time I enrolled in the Academy for

the Advanced Aviator because I wanted to be on the Pink Angels team? The instructor said I wasn't Pink Angel material because I enjoyed soaring and sightseeing the tropical scenery way more than learning the mechanics of velocity and speed. I didn't earn the certificate, and that's okay too. I took a chance at failing again, and that's how a flamingo, or a human, learns.

It sounds like quite a flock of flamingo flops, eh? Failures, some would even say. Hmm.

I offer a question for consideration, "humanhopper."

Were those flops, indeed, failures? I know better when I look back in tailfeather sight as the wizened flamingo I am now. However, during those earlier years, when it felt like I was flamingo flopping into every watery situation or experience I attempted, it began to take a toll. Now, I know great rewards often arrive in disguise, so I would pick my pink-plumed body up off the ground, shake out my tail feathers, and continue to webb-foot walk forward, but there was a time, I admit, that it affected my pink bird heart in ways I didn't expect.

Weeks passed, sunrise & sunset, tide ebb & tide flow. I almost didn't recognize the pink-plumed flamingo reflection each time I waded in the liquid coolness at day's end. My pink feathers had paled. I began to believe every flamingo flop defined me as less than all other flamingoes in my flamboyance. Alas, I was losing sight of the most critical flamingo lesson one can learn: balance.

Until one warm eve when my grandflamingo's words rippled through the tropical air: *One must always remain well-balanced and prepared for a potential splash before takeoff because you will not always achieve the perfect swan dive from an aqua-ed adventure.* (And, yes, I give credit where it is due — those swans have that dive thing perfected!)

When had I lost sight of that?

I was turning into a fla ... flamin ... flamingoer; a flamingoer stuck in the suctioned muck of chronic flamingoing behavior.

And that's never a good quality whether you are a flamingo or a human.

Hey, it's high tide.

Time for the deep dive.

"If you're not failing, you're probably not really moving forward."

— JOHN C. MAXWELL

**Lesson #6:** One can move forward only if one has both feet in (literally or mentally).

# *FLAMINGOER
## FLƏ•MÍŊ•GŌ•ƏR (NOUN)

A preened bird of pink-plumed perfectness that has become overly comfortable in constant flamin-going behavior to the detriment of forwarding life movement. Key behavioral patterns appear to develop from various life factors and false perceptions that failure means anything other than a falling ahead in life or a first attempt in the learning experience, pink feathers, and all.

Recognizable behaviors of a flamingoer may include bouts of avoidance, hesitancy, resistance to change, and, eventually, potential lifelong, pink-feathered inertia.

# THE FEARFUL FLAMINGOER
## CATALYST FOR CHANGE

It snuck in like a two-web-footed stealthy pink feathered ninja bird on a mission; the fear, the hesitation, the reluctance, the stuck in the algae-laden muck inertia. I was miserable. I didn't realize to what extent until that one day, one year ago, when I stood gazing out the office window, and I became aware that I stood perched on one sole webbed foot.

I had grown resistant to just about everything. I wasn't sure about relationships. I had grown hesitant to try new things, was afraid to follow my passions, and dreaded the "FAIL." Now, don't get me wrong. It wasn't some instantaneous revelation. I knew I had some flamingo flops that had pierced my feather-encased ego in the preceding years, but I didn't realize how deeply until that moment. Yes, I had become a pink-plumed, single-web-footed, standing flamingoer, and if a piled-high plate of plankton would be the grand prize for being the best, then I was due a full belly.

My mind waded back through time. When did it happen? What happened to the self-assured, flamazing, pastel-feathered flamingo I knew was hiding under these pink plumes? How did I get stuck in this whirlpool of self-defeating inertia? How had I fooled the other flamingos in the flamboyance for so long? Most importantly, how had I fooled myself?

Well, perch yourself on that rock and allow me to share.

It was an envied job for many here in my pink-feathered world: Marketing and Promotion Assistant at Agua di Avi. The pay was great, and I strutted home to my nest each payday with a stack of green bills tucked under my wings. The hefty salary allowed me to line my feathered abode with everything a single flamingo needed or wanted, or so it seemed.

I was also great at projecting a strategically manufactured outward appearance. I had an image to maintain, you know. It comes with the territory, right? With money comes power, with power comes status, and with status comes everything else. That's a life to "envy," correct? My feathered friends would come over to flock together, and my nest quickly became *the* "place to be."

It was all an illusion, though.

I was miserable. I didn't realize how miserable it was until one day, as I stood gazing out the office window, I became aware that one webbed foot had tucked itself deep into the comfort of feathered indecision and change reluctance.

Being the Marketing and Promotion Assistant at Aqua di Avi was a great "job." It just wasn't a genuine representation of the flamingo I was and wanted to be. Great pay notwithstanding, I didn't walk into that High Rise office nest every dawn with pulsating passion pumping through my veins. And I wanted to feel the rush of rose-colored passion pumping through my veins again!

I once again had allowed "comfort" and imagined

"safety" to take precedence, fully and completely, over living my life. I knew there was a greater purpose for my existence as an exquisite and dazzling bird with popping pink feathers, and I knew what it was.

So, what was I doing, and why?

Over the following two weeks, many deep dives occurred internally and physically. I needed to clear my avian mind and recalibrate my life goals. I faced my reluctance to make changes and found myself overthinking many possible disaster scenarios. It was a whirlpool that led to the proverbial watery "rabbit hole." (Okay, yes, I borrowed a favored human phrase) What if I followed my dreams and experienced a significant life Flamingo Flop? I held imaginary debates; miniature "me" flamingos, each holding space on a wing blade, honking out their best argument of pink persuasion until it all made perfect sense!

Exactly two weeks from that day of balancing, one-legged, looking out the office window, I stood outside Floyd Flamingo Sr.'s office with my letter of resignation tucked beneath my wing. My neck craned in nervous anticipation, and low nasal grunts threatened to escalate my lengthy esophagus. My feathers began ruffling like gusty winds were aloft, yet no air moved. However, the feeling of my webbed foot beginning its ascent towards "life-not-fully-lived" comfort and my mother's words ringing inside my head made me strut two-footed through the door. I looked at Floyd Flamingo Sr., staring at me with a beak slightly parted in surprise, reached out with my letter-held wing, laid the letter on the polished stone desk, and began living a life that was "authentically me."

Finally.

Both Feet In.

Was it scary? A little.

Okay, quite a bit.

But life isn't supposed to be boring, and "scary" is a fear we've usually mislabeled. It was more of a yet-to-be-experienced, eager excitement of the unknown.

Was it risky? You can bet your human behind it was.

I had to move from my fancy feathered nest; however, I relocated to a newly discovered watery location with a beautiful horizon view.

Was it worth it? It's more precious than a gold-plated, diamond-blinged-out treasure chest of pink flamingo feathers, and you can only imagine the price tag on that!!

"What's that?"

I'll be back in a moment, human.

## *FLAMAZING
FLƏ•MÁ•ZIŊG (ADJ)

very single, wondrously-unique, pink-feathered, two-legged flamingo ... flops included!
And YOU!!

"Fear is only as deep as the mind."

— JAPANESE PROVERB

# FOREVER FINE-FEATHERED & FLAMAZING

Sorry for the interruption. These four little flaminglets are always up to something, and the nesting partner needed a wing in the kitchen. Can you smell the aroma of seaweed-wrapped shrimp and sauteed plankton in the air? I would invite you for dinner, but I know your stay here is limited.

See, my friend, you and I aren't so different. Okay, besides the feathers, beak, brilliant hue, and some minor nuances of communication. If you want to live life fully, your wings must remain open to the waves of change and chance, risk and reward, flop and smooth landing. It doesn't matter if your days are spent in a watery lagoon or on *terra firma*. You miss all the excitement if you don't ride the wave for fear of falling in.

Take the chance and follow your dreams. Pursue your passions.

You are Flamazing.

Life is Flamazing, but only if you live it ... Both Feet In!

## *Both Feet In* Glossary
## Webb-sters Dictionary of Flamingo World Terminology

### *Life Edition*

**Flamazing/ Flə•má•ziŋg** (*adj*) Every single, wondrously unique, pink-feathered, two-legged flamingo...flops included!

**Flamingling/ Flə•míŋ•gliŋ** (*verb*) Every connection with other webbed puffs of pink throughout all life stages. Interflamingling and intraflamingling interactions encompass all approaches to communicating with similar species and involve flamingo-alized nasal honks, variations of pastel wing flapping, and slight nuances in neck-craning. One's flamingling behavior is entirely dependent, influenced, and affected by the many dives and dips taken in the ever-changing waters found in Life Lagoon.

**Flamingo/ Flə•míŋ•gō** (*noun*) A bird extraordinaire. Avian specimen of pink perfection. Exemplification of balance and poise. Portrayer of glitz and fun. "Spokesbird" for all things tropical, sunny, and warm. Utilized as an adornment for celebratory occasions and just about anything else the human species can conceive. In other words, the envy of the avian world, and rightfully so.

**Flamingoed/ Flə•míŋ•gōd** (*verb*) This "unpleasant" event occurs when the churning waters appear to relentlessly refuse to provide a calm and ripple-free haven for maintaining a secure flamingo balance regardless of putting your best foot forward. These unfortunate yet unavoidable occurrences will repeatedly happen during a flamingo's lifespan and occur in the work pond, during goal-seeking, within pink puff flamingo relationships, and when the tropical skies turn stormy for no apparent reason. Sometimes triggers a desire to throw pink wings up in the air and shuffle swiftly into the Pond of Pity. Sometimes leads to an unexpected Flamingo Flop. Although many pink flamingos view being flamingoed as a negative and unwanted cloud of frustration, these same two-legged balancers are often surprised by the hidden pastel lining.

Flamingoer/ Flə•mín•gō•ər (*noun*) A preened bird of pink-plumed perfectness who has become overly comfortable in constant flamingoing behavior to the detriment of forwarding life movement. Key behavioral patterns appear to develop from various life factors and false perception that failure means anything other than a Falling Ahead in Life or a First Attempting Learning experience, pink feathers, and all. Recognizable behaviors of a flamingoer may include episodes of avoidance, hesitancy, resistance to change, and, eventually, potential lifelong pink-feathered inertia.

Flamingo Flop / Flə•mín•gō Fläp (*noun*) An unavoidable life event that happens to all species members at some point if living life in forwarding motion. A natural result of taking chances. This can occur at any time and may occur within many life dynamics, including rela-

*BOTH FEET IN:*

tionship-seeking, skill-building, business ventures, or when one is willing and daring enough to seek new adventures. Happens when the imagined smooth "*that* deserves a 10" ripple-free swan dive into clear waters becomes an unexpected belly flop into unfamiliar waters, most often resulting in an unanticipated watery mess. Sometimes used as an excuse for sedentary flamingoing or flamingoer behavior. Masquerades as some of the most valuable feather-earning life lessons a flamingo can experience, such that recognition of the downside risk(s) may deliver full flamingo maturity status.

Flamingoing/ Flə•míŋ•gō•iŋg (*verb*) The expected avian behavior for all flamingo flock members. An innate propensity to remain in the one-legged stance of comfortable familiarity for long periods. Collective and societal patterning of unnecessary movement resistance once a graceful one-legged balance occurs unless necessary for fundamental provisions and daily flamingo interaction. This behavior ensures warmth retention, a sense of familiar comfort, and conservation of energy spent on unnecessary movement. As with all behavioral patterns, flamingoing may become problematic if resistance to forward movement occurs due to fear of failure, past negative experiences, and reluctance to take chances, resulting in missing out on full-spectrum living, an event undesirable for all species, feathered or not.

# LESSONS LEARNED

Lesson #1: Remaining in stagnant waters affects emotional and physical health. Besides, it may entirely dim one's brilliant plumage!

Lesson #2: The most priceless flamingo feathers are those obtained through consistent resurfacing after life's unexpected splashes.

Lesson #3: When life tosses you a lemon, remember, nothing tastes sweeter than a coconut shell full of pink lemonade .... oh, and top it off with a tropical-looking drink umbrella!

Lesson #4: It's just a matter of adjusting your wings ... oops ... sails.

. . .

**L**esson #5: Sometimes, the most valuable pearls hide inside the roughest clams.

**L**esson #6: One can move forward only if one has both feet in (literally or mentally).

Both Feet In. Always. Every day. No excuses.

# 1

# TEN FUN FACTS ABOUT THE AMAZING FLAMINGO

- Flamingos gather their food by turning their heads upside down in the water. NOT recommended for human consumption!
- Although I have taken the liberty of remarking about the flamingo's knobby knees, they are knobby-ankled. Their knees are much higher and hidden under their feathers.
- Who copies who? A flamingo bends its legs just like humans do.
- Both Mom and Dad produce the milk for their little ones. That's what I call actual shared parenting!
- The milk for those little ones is produced in a part of the throat and fed through the parent's mouth.
- Although few people see it happen, flamingos genuinely fly.
- Flamingos can sleep while standing on one leg. I prefer a nice comfy bed!

- Flamingos live for approximately twenty to thirty years on average.
- Just as we humans develop friend relationships with those sharing similar personalities, the flamingos do as well.
- It is a diet of algae and brine shrimp, helping to create the popping pink color of our flamingo friend.

# ABOUT THE AUTHOR

Patti Ann resides in a quaint little northeast Ohio town surrounded by the flamingos...oops...humans she loves the most. Daily appreciative of the gift of readable word juggling, the author's singular goal is to leave her readers with a smile and joy in their hearts.

And as to the passion of my pink flamingo friend, it seems we share another commonality, and when I last checked in, he still had a pink plumed feather pen tucked in his wing and an even wider smile on his beak.

I hope you enjoyed spending time with our pink feathered friends in BOTH FEET IN: NAVIGATING LIFE IN A FLAMINGO WORLD.

Please don't forget to leave a review, and may all your journeys be taken with...
Both Feet In.

www.ingramcontent.com/pod-product-compliance
Lightning Source LLC
Chambersburg PA
CBHW071324040426
42444CB00009B/2073